Thank you so much for trying our gratitude journal! We'd love to hear from you!

If you have some super ideas for topics or books, please email us. Podchilla LOVES to get email from her readers.

If you've found this to be a good journal, please leave us a HAPPY REVIEW! We LOVE happy people!

If you have any trouble with this product, please email us and we will do our best make it right.

Send Email To: podchilla@gmail.com

Happy Journaling!

Use this section to get ideas on how to spread kindness throughout your day. At the end of the day, write down how you performed an act of kindness.

This section helps you to get ideas and has positive and uplifting thoughts.

Try to fill at least one item before starting your day. If you have more, then write them down. You can also add more after your day is over.

Do this section before you go to bed. Reflect on the day and try to find the good even if your day wasn't so good.

 Happy

 Silly

 Worried

 Sad

 Embarrassed

 Angry

Today's Date:

It's Cool To Be Kind! 💡 idea Pick Up Litter

How Was I Kind Today?

Name A Person You're Thankful For

Today I'm Grateful For:

_____

_____

_____

_____

The Best Part Of My Day Was:

_____

_____

_____

_____

How I Feel Today:

Today's Date:

It's Cool To Be Kind!   Hold the door for someone

How Was I Kind Today?

Name Something Outside You Are Thankful For

Today I'm Grateful For:

_____

_____

_____

_____

The Best Part Of My Day Was:

_____

_____

_____

_____

How I Feel Today:

Today's Date:

It's Cool To Be Kind!　　　💡 Leave change in the vending machine

How Was I Kind Today?

Name Something Inside You Are Thankful For

Today I'm Grateful For:

_____

_____

_____

_____

The Best Part Of My Day Was:

_____

_____

_____

_____

How I Feel Today:

Today's Date:

It's Cool To Be Kind! 💡 idea   Tell A Joke

How Was I Kind Today?

What Is A Skill You're Thankful For?

😌 Today I'm Grateful For:

_____

_____

_____

_____

😁 The Best Part Of My Day Was:

_____

_____

_____

_____

How I Feel Today:

Today's Date:

It's Cool To Be Kind! :idea: Leave A Note In A Library Book

How Was I Kind Today?

You Are An Amazing Person

Today I'm Grateful For:

_____
_____
_____
_____

The Best Part Of My Day Was:

_____
_____
_____
_____

How I Feel Today:

Today's Date:

It's Cool To Be Kind!　idea　Return the Shopping Cart

How Was I Kind Today?

Name Something Fun You Are Thankful For

Today I'm Grateful For:

_____

_____

_____

_____

The Best Part Of My Day Was:

_____

_____

_____

_____

How I Feel Today:

Today's Date:

It's Cool To Be Kind! 💡 idea   Give Candy To Someone

How Was I Kind Today?

Name Something Beautiful You Are Thankful For

Today I'm Grateful For:

_____

_____

_____

_____

The Best Part Of My Day Was:

_____

_____

_____

_____

How I Feel Today:

Today's Date:

It's Cool To Be Kind! 💡 Let someone go in front of you in line

How Was I Kind Today?

Name A Teacher You Are Thankful For

😌 Today I'm Grateful For:

_____

_____

_____

_____

😀 The Best Part Of My Day Was:

_____

_____

_____

_____

How I Feel Today:

Today's Date:

It's Cool To Be Kind! 💡 Say "hi" to someone new

How Was I Kind Today?

I Forgive Myself For Mistakes

😌 Today I'm Grateful For:

_____

_____

_____

_____

😁 The Best Part Of My Day Was:

_____

_____

_____

_____

How I Feel Today:

Today's Date:

It's Cool To Be Kind!   Do A Chore Without Being Asked

How Was I Kind Today?

Name Something That Makes You Laugh

Today I'm Grateful For:

_____

_____

_____

_____

The Best Part Of My Day Was:

_____

_____

_____

_____

How I Feel Today:

Today's Date:

It's Cool To Be Kind!   Help Someone Else Do Their Chores

How Was I Kind Today?

Name A Sad Thing That Happened, But That You Learned From

Today I'm Grateful For:

_____

_____

_____

_____

The Best Part Of My Day Was:

_____

_____

_____

_____

How I Feel Today:

Today's Date:

It's Cool To Be Kind!   Give A Genuine Compliment

How Was I Kind Today?

It's Okay Not To Know Everything

Today I'm Grateful For:

_____

_____

_____

_____

The Best Part Of My Day Was:

_____

_____

_____

_____

How I Feel Today:

Today's Date:

It's Cool To Be Kind!   Plant A Tree

How Was I Kind Today?

Name Something That You Love To Smell

Today I'm Grateful For:

_____

_____

_____

_____

The Best Part Of My Day Was:

_____

_____

_____

_____

How I Feel Today:

Today's Date:

It's Cool To Be Kind! 💡 idea   Make Cookies To Share

How Was I Kind Today?

What Was Your Favorite Gift You Received?

😌 Today I'm Grateful For:

_____

_____

_____

_____

😁 The Best Part Of My Day Was:

_____

_____

_____

_____

How I Feel Today:

Today's Date:

It's Cool To Be Kind! 💡 When Someone Is Talking, Put Down Your Phone

How Was I Kind Today?

I Can Make A Difference

☺ Today I'm Grateful For:

_____

_____

_____

_____

☺ The Best Part Of My Day Was:

_____

_____

_____

_____

How I Feel Today:

Use This Space To Doodle Some Thoughts!

Today's Date:

It's Cool To Be Kind! 💡 idea   Offer To Walk Someone's Dog

How Was I Kind Today?

What Is Something In Your Room You're Thankful For?

Today I'm Grateful For:

_____

_____

_____

_____

The Best Part Of My Day Was:

_____

_____

_____

_____

How I Feel Today:

Today's Date:

It's Cool To Be Kind!　　☀idea　　Offer To Pet Sit

How Was I Kind Today?

Name A Pet You Are Thankful For

Today I'm Grateful For:

_____

_____

_____

_____

The Best Part Of My Day Was:

_____

_____

_____

_____

How I Feel Today:

Today's Date:

It's Cool To Be Kind!   Offer To Volunteer At The Animal Shelter

How Was I Kind Today?

Name A Favorite Book

Today I'm Grateful For:

_____

_____

_____

_____

The Best Part Of My Day Was:

_____

_____

_____

_____

How I Feel Today:

Today's Date:

It's Cool To Be Kind! 💡 idea Wash Someone's Car

How Was I Kind Today?

All Of My Problems Have Solutions

Today I'm Grateful For:

_____
_____
_____
_____

The Best Part Of My Day Was:

_____
_____
_____
_____

How I Feel Today:

Today's Date:

It's Cool To Be Kind! 💡 Sell Something And Donate The Profits

How Was I Kind Today?

What Are Some Qualities You Love About Yourself?

Today I'm Grateful For:

_____

_____

_____

_____

The Best Part Of My Day Was:

_____

_____

_____

_____

How I Feel Today:

Today's Date:

It's Cool To Be Kind! 💡 Send A Card To A Service Member

How Was I Kind Today?

What Is Something You'd Like To Improve On?

😌 Today I'm Grateful For:

_____

_____

_____

_____

😁 The Best Part Of My Day Was:

_____

_____

_____

_____

How I Feel Today: 😁 😝 😳 😔 😠 😡

Today's Date:

It's Cool To Be Kind! 💡 Tell Someone They Are Special

How Was I Kind Today?

My Mistakes Help Me Learn And Grow

😌 Today I'm Grateful For:

_____

_____

_____

_____

😁 The Best Part Of My Day Was:

_____

_____

_____

_____

How I Feel Today:

Today's Date:

It's Cool To Be Kind! 💡 idea   Buy A Drink For A Friend

How Was I Kind Today?

What Is Your Favorite Time Of The Day?

😌 Today I'm Grateful For:

_____

_____

_____

_____

😃 The Best Part Of My Day Was:

_____

_____

_____

_____

How I Feel Today: 😁 😝 😳 😎 🤙 😠

Today's Date:

It's Cool To Be Kind!   Set The Table For Dinner

How Was I Kind Today?

What Is Your Favorite Animal?

Today I'm Grateful For:

The Best Part Of My Day Was:

How I Feel Today:

Today's Date:

It's Cool To Be Kind!   Bury A Treasure At The Playground

How Was I Kind Today?

What Would Be Your Dream Job?

Today I'm Grateful For:

_____

_____

_____

_____

The Best Part Of My Day Was:

_____

_____

_____

_____

How I Feel Today:

Today's Date:

😎 It's Cool To Be Kind! 💡 Donate Some Clothes To Kids Who Need Them

How Was I Kind Today?

Name Something You Love About Your Mom or Dad

😌 Today I'm Grateful For:

_____

_____

_____

_____

😃 The Best Part Of My Day Was:

_____

_____

_____

_____

How I Feel Today:

Today's Date:

😎 It's Cool To Be Kind! 🔅 idea Pass Out Some Fun Stickers

How Was I Kind Today?

I Have People Who Love And Respect Me

😌 Today I'm Grateful For:

_____

_____

_____

_____

😁 The Best Part Of My Day Was:

_____

_____

_____

_____

How I Feel Today: 😁 😋 😳 😎 🤙 😠

Today's Date:

It's Cool To Be Kind! 💡 Talk To Someone New At School

How Was I Kind Today?

What Color Are You Thankful For?

😌 Today I'm Grateful For:

_____

_____

_____

_____

😃 The Best Part Of My Day Was:

_____

_____

_____

_____

How I Feel Today:

Today's Date:

It's Cool To Be Kind!   💡 idea   Don't Allow People To Be Bullied

How Was I Kind Today?

I Can Do Anything I Put My Mind To

😌 Today I'm Grateful For:

_____

_____

_____

_____

😁 The Best Part Of My Day Was:

_____

_____

_____

_____

How I Feel Today: 😁 😜 😳 😎 🤙 😠

Use This Space To Doodle Some Thoughts!

Today's Date:

😎 It's Cool To Be Kind!　💡 idea　Donate To The Food Pantry

How Was I Kind Today?

What Holiday Are You Thankful For?

😌 Today I'm Grateful For:

_____

_____

_____

_____

😁 The Best Part Of My Day Was:

_____

_____

_____

_____

How I Feel Today:

Today's Date:

It's Cool To Be Kind!   idea   Bring Flowers For A Teacher

How Was I Kind Today?

What Texture Are You Thankful For?

Today I'm Grateful For:

_____

_____

_____

_____

The Best Part Of My Day Was:

_____

_____

_____

_____

How I Feel Today:

Today's Date:

It's Cool To Be Kind! 💡 idea Tell A Server How Great Their Service Wa

How Was I Kind Today?

Name Something You Saw You Were Thankful For

Today I'm Grateful For:

_____
_____
_____
_____

The Best Part Of My Day Was:

_____
_____
_____
_____

How I Feel Today:

Today's Date:

It's Cool To Be Kind!   Take Treats To The Fire Station

How Was I Kind Today?

What Season Are You Thankful For?

Today I'm Grateful For:

_____

_____

_____

_____

The Best Part Of My Day Was:

_____

_____

_____

_____

How I Feel Today:

Today's Date:

It's Cool To Be Kind! 💡idea Hug Someone

How Was I Kind Today?

What Is Your Favorite Part Of School This Year?

😌 Today I'm Grateful For:

_____

_____

_____

_____

😁 The Best Part Of My Day Was:

_____

_____

_____

_____

How I Feel Today:

Today's Date:

It's Cool To Be Kind! 💡 Say Thank You When Someone Is Kind

How Was I Kind Today?

What Are Your Goals For The Summer?

Today I'm Grateful For:

_____

_____

_____

_____

The Best Part Of My Day Was:

_____

_____

_____

_____

How I Feel Today:

Today's Date:

😎 It's Cool To Be Kind!　💡 Donate To Toys For Tots
idea

How Was I Kind Today?

Name Something New You Learned This Week

😌 Today I'm Grateful For:

_____

_____

_____

_____

😁 The Best Part Of My Day Was:

_____

_____

_____

_____

How I Feel Today:　😁　😛　😟　😣　🤙　😠

Today's Date:

It's Cool To Be Kind!　　💡 idea　Help Make Dinner

How Was I Kind Today?

Which Of Your 5 Senses Are You Most Grateful For?

Today I'm Grateful For:

_____

_____

_____

_____

The Best Part Of My Day Was:

_____

_____

_____

_____

How I Feel Today:

Today's Date:

It's Cool To Be Kind! 💡 idea Make A Get Well Card For Someone Sick

How Was I Kind Today?

Name A Person Who Helped You With A Problem

Today I'm Grateful For:

_____

_____

_____

_____

The Best Part Of My Day Was:

_____

_____

_____

_____

How I Feel Today:

Today's Date:

It's Cool To Be Kind! 💡 Clean Your Room Without Being Asked

How Was I Kind Today?

What Are You Looking Forward To This Week?

😌 Today I'm Grateful For:

_____
_____
_____
_____

😁 The Best Part Of My Day Was:

_____
_____
_____
_____

How I Feel Today: 😁 😝 😵 😎 🤙 😠

Today's Date:

It's Cool To Be Kind! 💡 Leave Kindness Stones In The Park

How Was I Kind Today?

What Makes You Feel Happy When You're Sad?

Today I'm Grateful For:

_____

_____

_____

_____

The Best Part Of My Day Was:

_____

_____

_____

_____

How I Feel Today:

Today's Date:

It's Cool To Be Kind!   Deliever Water Bottles To A Homeless Shelter

How Was I Kind Today?

When You're Sad, What Can Someone Say To Make You Feel Better?
(Remember this works for other's too!)

Today I'm Grateful For:

_____

_____

_____

_____

The Best Part Of My Day Was:

_____

_____

_____

_____

How I Feel Today:

Today's Date:

😎 It's Cool To Be Kind! 💡 Make A Homemade Gift For Someone

How Was I Kind Today?

What Is Your Biggest Talent?

😌 Today I'm Grateful For:

_____

_____

_____

_____

😃 The Best Part Of My Day Was:

_____

_____

_____

_____

How I Feel Today:

Today's Date:

It's Cool To Be Kind!   Smile At Everybody!
(It's Contagious!)

How Was I Kind Today?

All Of My Problems Have Solutions

Today I'm Grateful For:

_____
_____
_____
_____

The Best Part Of My Day Was:

_____
_____
_____
_____

How I Feel Today:

Use This Space To Doodle Some Thoughts!

Today's Date:

It's Cool To Be Kind!   Eat Lunch With The New Kid

How Was I Kind Today?

I Stand Up For What I Believe In

☺ Today I'm Grateful For:

_____

_____

_____

_____

☺ The Best Part Of My Day Was:

_____

_____

_____

_____

How I Feel Today:

Today's Date:

It's Cool To Be Kind! 🔆 Offer To Give A Dog A Bath

How Was I Kind Today?

Remember A Time When You Were Scared. How Did You Get Through It?

😌 Today I'm Grateful For:

_____

_____

_____

_____

😃 The Best Part Of My Day Was:

_____

_____

_____

How I Feel Today: 😁 😛 😳 😎 🤙 😠

Today's Date:

It's Cool To Be Kind! 💡 Send A Note To A Senior Citizen

How Was I Kind Today?

If A Genie Granted You 3 Wishes, What Would You Wish For?

Today I'm Grateful For:

_____

_____

_____

_____

The Best Part Of My Day Was:

_____

_____

_____

_____

How I Feel Today:

Today's Date:

It's Cool To Be Kind! 💡 idea Chew With Your Mouth Closed

How Was I Kind Today?

If You Could Have ONE Superpower, What Would It Be?

Today I'm Grateful For:

_____

_____

_____

_____

The Best Part Of My Day Was:

_____

_____

_____

_____

How I Feel Today:

Today's Date:

😎 It's Cool To Be Kind! 💡 idea Be On Time

How Was I Kind Today?

My Confidence Grows When I Step Out Of My Comfort Zone

😌 Today I'm Grateful For:

_____

_____

_____

_____

😁 The Best Part Of My Day Was:

_____

_____

_____

_____

How I Feel Today:

Today's Date:

It's Cool To Be Kind!   💡 idea   Be Clean

How Was I Kind Today?

What Is Your Favorite Kind Of Music?

😌 Today I'm Grateful For:

_____

_____

_____

_____

😄 The Best Part Of My Day Was:

_____

_____

_____

_____

How I Feel Today:

Today's Date:

☻ It's Cool To Be Kind! 🔆 Use A Napkin When Eating

How Was I Kind Today?

I Have The Power To Make My Dreams Come True

☺ Today I'm Grateful For:

_____
_____
_____
_____

☺ The Best Part Of My Day Was:

_____
_____
_____
_____

How I Feel Today:

Today's Date:

It's Cool To Be Kind! 💡 Try A New Food Even If You Aren't Sure You'll Like It

How Was I Kind Today?

What Opportunity Are You Thankful For?

😌 Today I'm Grateful For:

_____

_____

_____

_____

😁 The Best Part Of My Day Was:

_____

_____

_____

_____

How I Feel Today: 😁 😋 😵 😎 🤲 😠

Today's Date:

😎 It's Cool To Be Kind!　💡idea　Don't Burp In Someone's Face

How Was I Kind Today?

Every Day Is A Fresh Start

😌 Today I'm Grateful For:

_____

_____

_____

_____

😁 The Best Part Of My Day Was:

_____

_____

_____

_____

How I Feel Today:　😁　😝　😳　😎　🤙　😠

Today's Date:

It's Cool To Be Kind! 💡 Help With The Dinner Dishes

How Was I Kind Today?

What Can You Do To Be A Better Friend?

😌 Today I'm Grateful For:

_____

_____

_____

_____

😁 The Best Part Of My Day Was:

_____

_____

_____

_____

How I Feel Today:

Today's Date:

It's Cool To Be Kind! 💡 Forgive Someone Who Was Mean To You

How Was I Kind Today?

How Am I Better Today Than I Was Yesterday?

😌 Today I'm Grateful For:

_____

_____

_____

_____

😀 The Best Part Of My Day Was:

_____

_____

_____

_____

How I Feel Today:

Today's Date:

It's Cool To Be Kind!   idea   Reuse Grocery Bags

How Was I Kind Today?

Today I Will Walk Through My Fear

Today I'm Grateful For:

_____
_____
_____
_____

The Best Part Of My Day Was:

_____
_____
_____
_____

How I Feel Today:

Today's Date:

It's Cool To Be Kind! 💡 idea Get Some Exercise

How Was I Kind Today?

What Feature Do You Love About Your Body?

Today I'm Grateful For:

_____

_____

_____

_____

The Best Part Of My Day Was:

_____

_____

_____

_____

How I Feel Today:

Today's Date:

It's Cool To Be Kind! 💡 idea Start An Exercise Group

How Was I Kind Today?

Name A Time You Told Someone They Looked Good

Today I'm Grateful For:

_____

_____

_____

_____

The Best Part Of My Day Was:

_____

_____

_____

_____

How I Feel Today:

Use This Space To Doodle Some Thoughts!

Today's Date:

It's Cool To Be Kind! Call Your Grandparents. They Miss You

How Was I Kind Today?

Name Your Favorite Breakfast Food

Today I'm Grateful For:

_____

_____

_____

_____

The Best Part Of My Day Was:

_____

_____

_____

_____

How I Feel Today:

Today's Date:

It's Cool To Be Kind! 💡 Share Your Favorite Song

How Was I Kind Today?

What Is Your Favorite TV Show?

Today I'm Grateful For:

_____

_____

_____

_____

The Best Part Of My Day Was:

_____

_____

_____

_____

How I Feel Today:

Today's Date:

It's Cool To Be Kind! 💡 idea   Thank A Teacher

How Was I Kind Today?

What Is Your Favorite Weekend Activity?

😌 Today I'm Grateful For:

_____

_____

_____

_____

😁 The Best Part Of My Day Was:

_____

_____

_____

_____

How I Feel Today:

Today's Date:

It's Cool To Be Kind!   Offer To Do Yard Work

How Was I Kind Today?

What Is Your Favorite Funny Joke?

Today I'm Grateful For:

The Best Part Of My Day Was:

How I Feel Today:

Today's Date:

😎 It's Cool To Be Kind!　💡idea　Thank Your Bus Driver

How Was I Kind Today?

Name Something Hard You Achieved

😌 Today I'm Grateful For:

_____

_____

_____

_____

😃 The Best Part Of My Day Was:

_____

_____

_____

_____

How I Feel Today:

Today's Date:

It's Cool To Be Kind!   idea   Create A Bird Feeder

How Was I Kind Today?

What Do You Like Best About Your School?

Today I'm Grateful For:

_____

_____

_____

_____

The Best Part Of My Day Was:

_____

_____

_____

_____

How I Feel Today:

Today's Date:

It's Cool To Be Kind! 💡idea Get A Group Together To Pick Up Litter In The Par

How Was I Kind Today?

Name A Time You Helped Someone

Today I'm Grateful For:

_____
_____
_____
_____

The Best Part Of My Day Was:

_____
_____
_____
_____

How I Feel Today:

Today's Date:

It's Cool To Be Kind! Read A Book To A Senior Citizen

How Was I Kind Today?

Name A Way You Feel Most Loved

Today I'm Grateful For:

_____

_____

_____

_____

The Best Part Of My Day Was:

_____

_____

_____

_____

How I Feel Today:

Today's Date:

It's Cool To Be Kind! 🔆 Organize A Neighborhood Book Swap

How Was I Kind Today?

Have Courage And Confidence

😌 Today I'm Grateful For:

_____

_____

_____

_____

😀 The Best Part Of My Day Was:

_____

_____

_____

_____

How I Feel Today:

Today's Date:

It's Cool To Be Kind! 💡 idea Leave Post-It Notes On Lockers With Kind Words

How Was I Kind Today?

What Is An Event You're Thankful For?

Today I'm Grateful For:

_____

_____

_____

_____

The Best Part Of My Day Was:

_____

_____

_____

_____

How I Feel Today:

Today's Date:

It's Cool To Be Kind! 💡 idea   Share A Snack

How Was I Kind Today?

I Matter

😌 Today I'm Grateful For:

_____

_____

_____

_____

😁 The Best Part Of My Day Was:

_____

_____

_____

_____

How I Feel Today:

Today's Date:

It's Cool To Be Kind!   Recycle What You Can

How Was I Kind Today?

Name A Friend You Are Thankful For

Today I'm Grateful For:

_____

_____

_____

_____

The Best Part Of My Day Was:

_____

_____

_____

_____

How I Feel Today:

Use This Space To Doodle Some Thoughts!

Today's Date:

It's Cool To Be Kind!   Listen Without Interrupting

How Was I Kind Today?

Name A Favorite Movie

Today I'm Grateful For:

_____

_____

_____

_____

The Best Part Of My Day Was:

_____

_____

_____

_____

How I Feel Today:

Today's Date:

It's Cool To Be Kind!　　　idea　Encourage Other's To Try New Things

How Was I Kind Today?

If Someone Gave You A Gift You Didn't Like, How Would You Respond?

Today I'm Grateful For:

_____

_____

_____

_____

The Best Part Of My Day Was:

_____

_____

_____

_____

How I Feel Today:

Today's Date:

It's Cool To Be Kind! 💡idea Let Someone Know When They Are Being Helpfu

How Was I Kind Today?

Name Something You Are Proud Of

Today I'm Grateful For:

_____

_____

_____

_____

The Best Part Of My Day Was:

_____

_____

_____

_____

How I Feel Today:

Today's Date:

It's Cool To Be Kind! 💡idea Don't Gossip

How Was I Kind Today?

Where Was Your Favorite Vacation?

Today I'm Grateful For:

_____

_____

_____

_____

The Best Part Of My Day Was:

_____

_____

_____

_____

How I Feel Today:

Today's Date:

It's Cool To Be Kind! 💡 idea Make Breakfast For Yourself

How Was I Kind Today?

I Deserve To Be Loved

😌 Today I'm Grateful For:

_____

_____

_____

_____

😀 The Best Part Of My Day Was:

_____

_____

_____

_____

How I Feel Today:

Today's Date:

😎 It's Cool To Be Kind!   💡 Let Your Parents Sleep In
                              idea

How Was I Kind Today?

What Sound Are You Thankful For?

😌 Today I'm Grateful For:

_____

_____

_____

_____

😁 The Best Part Of My Day Was:

_____

_____

_____

_____

How I Feel Today: 😁   😝   😌   😔   🤙   😠

Today's Date:

It's Cool To Be Kind! 💡 idea Play With The Unpopular Kids

How Was I Kind Today?

Today I Choose To Be Confident

😌 Today I'm Grateful For:

_____

_____

_____

_____

😀 The Best Part Of My Day Was:

_____

_____

_____

_____

How I Feel Today:

Today's Date:

It's Cool To Be Kind!   Finish Homework Without Being Asked

How Was I Kind Today?

Who Is Your Favorite Superhero? Why?

Today I'm Grateful For:

_____

_____

_____

_____

The Best Part Of My Day Was:

_____

_____

_____

_____

How I Feel Today:

Today's Date:

It's Cool To Be Kind! Have A Root Beer Blast

How Was I Kind Today?

If You Could Change Something About The World, What Would It Be?

Today I'm Grateful For:

The Best Part Of My Day Was:

How I Feel Today:

Today's Date:

It's Cool To Be Kind!   Fold And Put Away Your Clothes

How Was I Kind Today?

I Accept Who I Am

☺ Today I'm Grateful For:

_____

_____

_____

_____

☺ The Best Part Of My Day Was:

_____

_____

_____

_____

How I Feel Today:

Today's Date:

😎 It's Cool To Be Kind! 💡 Don't Allow People To Be Mean

How Was I Kind Today?

What Is The Bravest Thing You've Ever Done?

😌 Today I'm Grateful For:

_____

_____

_____

_____

😁 The Best Part Of My Day Was:

_____

_____

_____

_____

How I Feel Today: 😁 😝 😳 😔 🤙 😠

Today's Date:

It's Cool To Be Kind! 💡idea Tell A Family Member How Much You Appreciate Them

How Was I Kind Today?

I Believe In Myself And My Abilities

Today I'm Grateful For:

_____

_____

_____

_____

The Best Part Of My Day Was:

_____

_____

_____

_____

How I Feel Today: 😁 😛 😳 😎 🤙 😠

Today's Date:

It's Cool To Be Kind! 💡 idea Go Outside And Leave Your Phone

How Was I Kind Today?

I Am Open And Ready To Learn

😌 Today I'm Grateful For:

_____
_____
_____
_____

😁 The Best Part Of My Day Was:

_____
_____
_____
_____

How I Feel Today:

Today's Date:

😎 It's Cool To Be Kind!　💡 idea　Talk To The Shy Person

How Was I Kind Today?

Name A Way You Showed Compassion

😌 Today I'm Grateful For:

_____

_____

_____

_____

😁 The Best Part Of My Day Was:

_____

_____

_____

_____

How I Feel Today:　😁　😝　😳　😌　😒　😠

Today's Date:

It's Cool To Be Kind! 💡idea Be Patient

How Was I Kind Today?

What Is A Luxury You Are Thankful For?

Today I'm Grateful For:

_____

_____

_____

_____

The Best Part Of My Day Was:

_____

_____

_____

_____

How I Feel Today:

Today's Date:

It's Cool To Be Kind! 💡 Make Two Lunches, Give One Away

How Was I Kind Today?

There Is No One Better To Be Than Myself

😌 Today I'm Grateful For:

_____

_____

_____

_____

😁 The Best Part Of My Day Was:

_____

_____

_____

_____

How I Feel Today: 😁 😋 😯 😔 🤙 😠

Today's Date:

It's Cool To Be Kind!   💡 idea   Share Your Umbrella

How Was I Kind Today?

What Is Your Favorite Hobby?

Today I'm Grateful For:

_____

_____

_____

_____

The Best Part Of My Day Was:

_____

_____

_____

_____

How I Feel Today:

Today's Date:

😎 It's Cool To Be Kind!　　💡 Loan Someone Your Favorite Book
idea

How Was I Kind Today?

I Am Enough

😌 Today I'm Grateful For:

_____

_____

_____

_____

😁 The Best Part Of My Day Was:

_____

_____

_____

_____

How I Feel Today:　😁 😛 😳 😎 🤙 😠

Today's Date:

It's Cool To Be Kind! 💡 idea Help With The Laundry

How Was I Kind Today?

Name Something You Love To Eat

😌 Today I'm Grateful For:

_____

_____

_____

_____

😁 The Best Part Of My Day Was:

_____

_____

_____

_____

How I Feel Today:

Today's Date:

😎 It's Cool To Be Kind!   💡 idea Draw A Picture For Your Teacher

How Was I Kind Today?

If I Fall, I Will Get Back Up Again

😌 Today I'm Grateful For:

_____

_____

_____

_____

😁 The Best Part Of My Day Was:

_____

_____

_____

_____

How I Feel Today: 😄 😝 😵 😎 🤙 😠

Today's Date:

😎 It's Cool To Be Kind!　　💡idea Tell Your Family You Love Them Every Day

How Was I Kind Today?

I Can Do Anything

😌 Today I'm Grateful For:

_____

_____

_____

_____

😁 The Best Part Of My Day Was:

_____

_____

_____

_____

How I Feel Today:

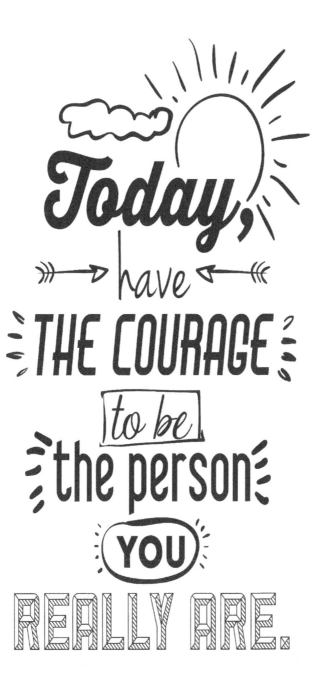

Made in the USA
Middletown, DE
17 March 2020